TAKE A CLOSER LOOK AT YOUR
Brain

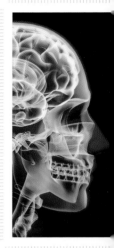

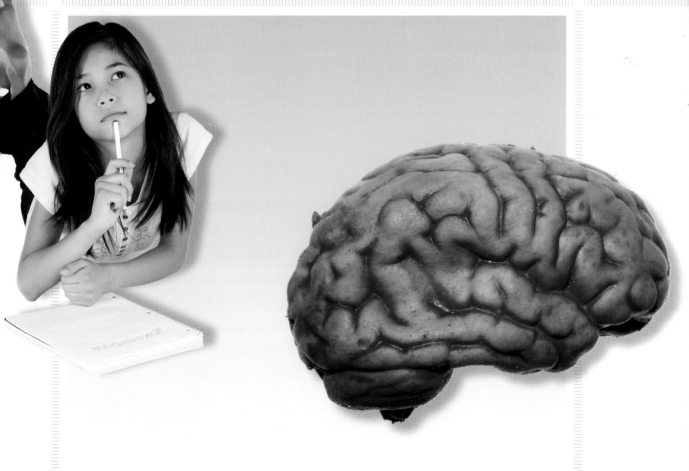

BY JANE P. GARDNER

The Child's World

Published by The Child's World®
1980 Lookout Drive • Mankato, MN 56003-1705
800-599-READ • www.childsworld.com

Acknowledgments
The Child's World®: Mary Berendes, Publishing Director
Red Line Editorial: Editorial direction and production
The Design Lab: Design
Content Consultant: Jeffrey W. Oseid, MD

Photographs ©: Leonello Calvetti/Shutterstock Images,
5; Jacek Chabraszewski/Shutterstock Images, 7, 24;
Shutterstock Images, 9, 14, 17, 18; Sebastian Kaulitzki/
iStockphoto, 10; Jaren Jai Wicklund/Shutterstock Images,
11; Andrii Muzyka/Shutterstock Images, 13; Monkey
Business Images/Shutterstock Images, 19; Yuri Arcurs/
Shutterstock Images, 21

Front cover: Shutterstock Images; Jaren Jai Wicklund/
Shutterstock Images

ISBN: 978-1623235499
LCCN: 2013931443

Printed in the United States of America
Mankato, MN
July, 2013
PA02175

About the Author
Jane P. Gardner is a freelance science writer with a master's degree in Geology. She worked as a science teacher for several years before becoming a science writer. She has written textbooks, tests, laboratory experiments, and other books on biology, health, environmental science, chemistry, geography, Earth science, and math.

Table of Contents

CHAPTER 1
Use Your Brain

Thinking, breathing, dreaming, talking, eating, running, writing. You might do all these things today. Each action is controlled by one organ in your body—the brain. The brain is the third largest organ in the body. It uses more energy than any of the other organs.

Some people think the brain looks like a bunch of cauliflower. It is soft, wrinkly, and gray. It sits in liquid inside your skull. An adult human brain weighs about 3 pounds (1.4 kg).

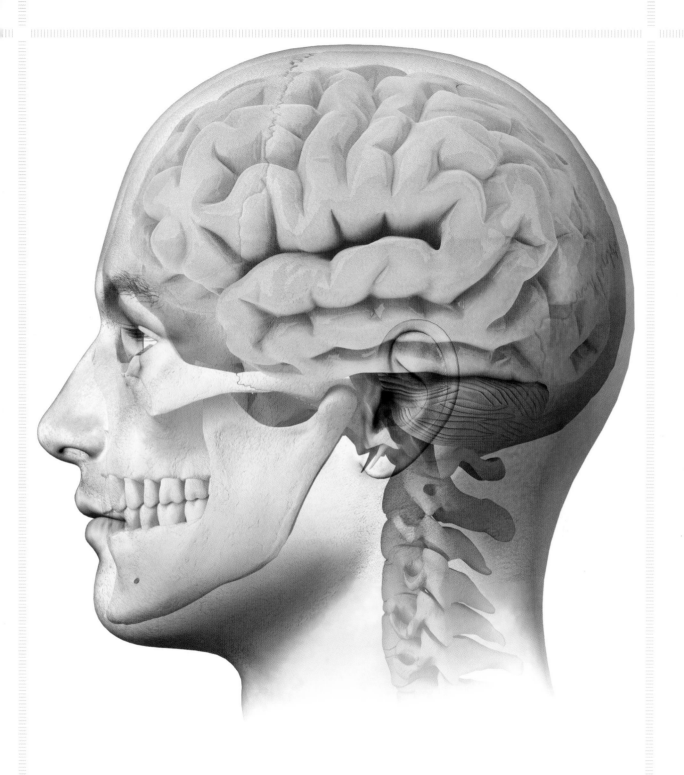

An adult brain is about as heavy as a cantaloupe.

The brain has three different parts. Each part controls different areas of your life. Some parts make you creative. Other parts help you walk and talk. Some parts of your brain keep your body at 98.6 degrees Fahrenheit (37 degrees Celsius).

Are you artsy and creative? Or are you more of a numbers person who likes things to be in order? Left-brain thinkers tend to be more orderly. Right-brain thinkers tend to be more artsy.

The **forebrain** is the largest part of the brain. It is in the front part of your skull. This is where the **cerebrum** is located. The cerebrum controls your thoughts. It also helps you memorize spelling words and solve math problems. A lot of thinking goes on in the forebrain.

The brain controls every action the body makes.

The smallest part of the brain is called the **midbrain**. The **brain stem** is part of the midbrain. The brain stem controls your breathing. It also makes sure your **involuntary** muscles do their job. These are the muscles that work all on their own. Your heart is an involuntary muscle. You do not have to think about your heart beating because it beats by itself.

Can you dribble a basketball or play the piano? You can do these things because of your **hindbrain**. The hindbrain is at the back of your skull. This part of the brain includes the **cerebellum**. The cerebellum controls the way your body moves. It helps you balance on a beam or sit up straight in your chair.

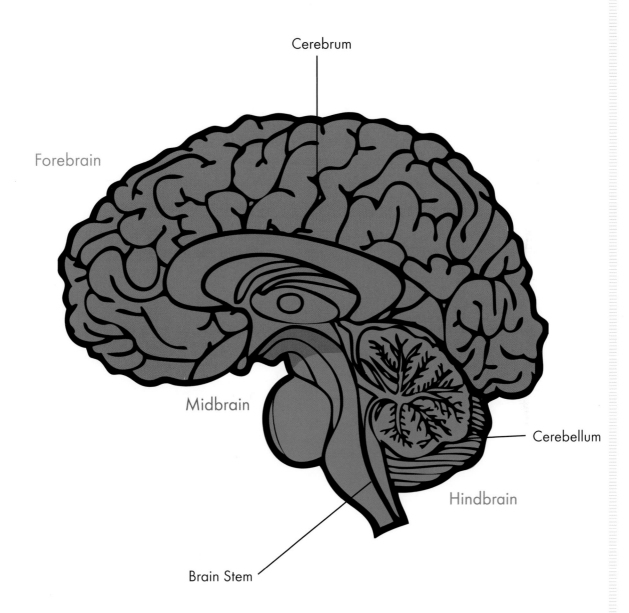

Cerebrum

Forebrain

Midbrain

Cerebellum

Hindbrain

Brain Stem

CHAPTER 2

What Does the Brain Do?

The brain and the spinal cord make up the **central nervous system**. Without them, you wouldn't be able to act or think.

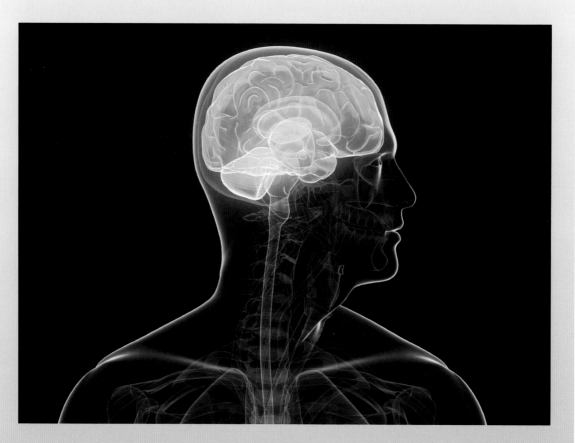

The brain and the spinal cord work together to control your actions and senses.

Neurons are like messengers to the central nervous system. The neurons collect information from different parts of the body. Then they bring these messages to your brain.

If you put your hand on something hot, the neurons in your hand send messages to your brain. The brain thinks about those messages and sends a message back to your hand. The message tells your hand to move off the hot object. All of this happens in less than one second.

Your brain has more than 100 billion neurons. Neurons help you balance on your bike and remember the words to your favorite song.

Neurons even help you with your homework.

Your brain helps you learn new things. Every time you learn something new, your brain changes a little bit. Maybe you wonder why your teacher always tells you to study. Or why your coach always tells you to practice. This is because practice teaches our brains how to do something new.

About 70,000 thoughts pass through your brain every day. Your brain keeps working even when you sleep.

Think of tying your shoes. You did not know how to tie them when you were younger. But after practicing, you now can tie your shoes almost without looking. Every time you practiced, your brain sent messages to your hands about tying your shoes. These messages traveled the same path over and over until you learned how to tie your shoes. Now your brain does not really have to think about it. Your brain already knows the "shoe-tying" path to follow.

Every time you learn something new, neurons in your brain connect and make more paths.

Problems with the Brain

The brain is inside your skull. An adult human skull is about 1/4 inch (7 mm) thick. A few layers of soft tissue and fluid are around the brain. The skull, layers of tissue, and fluid all help protect the brain from injuries.

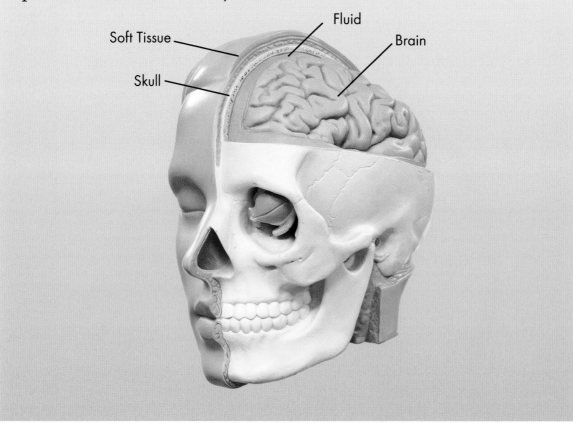

Fluid

Soft Tissue

Brain

Skull

You cannot break your brain like you can break an arm or your finger. But your brain can still get injured. A common brain injury is a **concussion**. This is when the brain moves inside the skull after a hit or a fall. Concussions can happen if you get hit too hard while playing football or if you take a bad fall off your bike. Someone with a concussion might feel confused, sleepy, or sick. Someone who might have a concussion should see a doctor right away.

Sometimes cells in the brain grow in weird ways. This can form a brain tumor. Most tumors cause problems. A tumor grows on a part of the brain. As it grows bigger, it pushes on the brain to try to make room for itself. The part the tumor is growing on can change. If a tumor is pushing on the part of the brain that helps you see, you may have trouble seeing.

When you have a headache, it is your head that hurts—not your brain. The brain cannot sense or feel any pain.

Healthy Brain

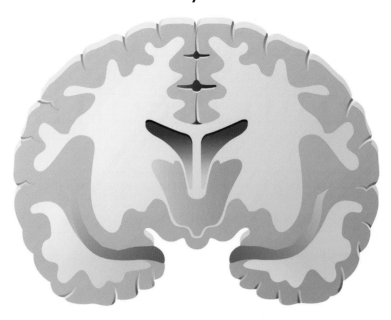

Brain with Tumor

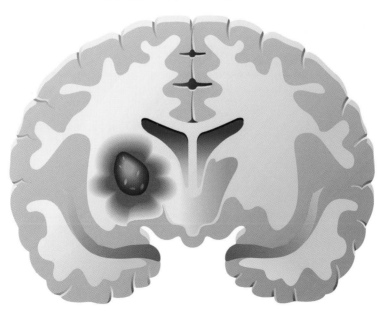

CHAPTER 4

Keep Your Brain Healthy

Everyone needs to keep his or her brain healthy and safe.
There are many ways to keep your brain in tip-top shape.

Blueberries are a tasty dark fruit to eat for a healthy brain.

Eat healthy foods. Fish is sometimes called "brain food." Fish, such as tuna and salmon, have chemicals that keep the brain healthy. Other foods that are good for the brain include dark fruits and vegetables, such as raisins and spinach. Nuts, such as walnuts, pecans, and almonds, are also part of a good diet for the brain.

Get plenty of exercise. Being active can help keep your brain in good shape. It is important to be safe when you exercise or play a sport. Always wear a helmet when riding a bike or a scooter. Make sure the helmet is the right size for your head. The straps should fit tight and snug under your chin.

A helmet can protect your brain from a fall.

Some poisons can damage the brain. **Carbon monoxide** is a gas you cannot see or smell. It can come from the gas we use for heaters or cars. It mixes in with the air we breathe. We are around small amounts of carbon monoxide all the time. But too much can damage the brain. Help keep the brains in your home healthy. Ask your parents to make sure gas heaters in your home are working as they should.

Get to bed early tonight. Studies show students do better on math problems with a good night's sleep.

Be curious about the world around you. Reading, writing, and playing games are all good things to do every day. Ask more questions. Learning new things and solving problems can help keep your brain healthy.

Exercise your brain by learning something new every day.

brain stem (BRAYN stem) The brain stem connects the brain to the spinal cord. It controls involuntary actions.

carbon monoxide (KAHR-buhn muh-nahk-side) Carbon monoxide is a poisonous gas made by vehicles and other things that burn fuel. Breathing in too much carbon monoxide can harm the brain.

central nervous system (SEN-truhl nur-vuhs sis-tuhm) The central nervous system is part of the nervous system. It is made up of the brain and the spinal cord.

cerebellum (SARE-uh-bell-uhm) The cerebellum is the part of the brain that helps with balance. The cerebellum is in the hindbrain.

cerebrum (SARE-ee-bruhm) The cerebrum controls body movement and collects information from the senses. The cerebrum is in the forebrain.

concussion (kuhn-KUHSH-uhn) A concussion is a brain injury caused by a hard hit to the head. During a concussion, the brain moves from side to side inside the skull.

forebrain (FOR-brayn) The largest part of the brain is the forebrain. The forebrain is in the front part of the skull and contains the cerebrum.

hindbrain (HINDE-brayn) The hindbrain is at the back of the skull. The hindbrain includes the cerebellum.

involuntary (in-VAH-luhn-tare-ee) To do something involuntary means it is done automatically or without control. The brain stem controls involuntary muscles.

midbrain (MID-brayn) The smallest part of the brain is the midbrain. The brain stem is part of the midbrain.

neurons (NOOR-ahnz) Neurons are cells that carry information between the brain and other body parts. More than 100 billion neurons in the brain work together to control the whole body.

BOOKS

Ballard, Carol. *The Brain and Nervous System*. Detroit, MI: KidHaven Press, 2005.

Newquist, H.P. *The Great Brain Book*. New York: Scholastic Reference, 2005.

Simon, Seymour. *The Brain: Our Nervous System*. New York: Harper Collins, 2006.

WEB SITES

Visit our Web site for links about the brain: **childsworld.com/links**

Note to Parents, Teachers, and Librarians: We routinely verify our Web links to make sure they are safe and active sites. So encourage your readers to check them out!

INDEX